C000145909

# THE STATUES
# OF EMO COURT

*in memory of my mother*
*Nancy Boran (1923–2020)*

# THE STATUES
# OF EMO COURT

*poem & images*
## PAT BORAN

Orange Crate Books

*The Statues of Emo Court* is first published in 2021
by Orange Crate Books, Dublin, Ireland.

Text and images copyright © Pat Boran, 2021

ISBN 978-0-9931726-4-9 (paperback)

Printed in Dublin by Print Dynamics.

Orange Crate Books are available
through Dedalus Press, Dublin, Ireland.
See *www.dedaluspress.com*

Located near the village of Emo, Co. Laois, Emo
Court is a neo-classical mansion with gardens, in
1994 presented to President Mary Robinson by its
then owner Major Cholmeley-Harrison, since when it has
been in the care of the Office of Public Works.

*The Statues of Emo Court* was originally conceived as a
poetry film, commissioned by Dunamaise Arts Centre,
Portlaoise, and published in November 2020. The text is
reproduced here in full. The images are taken from the film
which, together with other poetry films by the author, may
be seen at *www.patboran.com*.

# 1

CHILDREN ADORE THEM, adults seem blind,
the wildlife are all devotees:
the squirrels and beetles, the butterflies,
the crows that confer in the trees ...

Spiders spinning webs in their limbs,
moss on their shoulders and knees,
as if they were dreaming, the statues of Emo
are out here to practise Tai Chi.

DAYS AND NIGHTS are like tides on the move;
the light fades, then inky black
darkness advances, our bleakest thoughts
faces trapped behind glass.

Now the statues on their plinths of stone
are like pieces left behind
when some strange game of chess is abandoned —
games the last things on our minds …

Here, there, alone, together,
wounded they convalesce.
Whole worlds reduced to these small circles,
they remind us of ourselves.

Weeks turn to months, and overhead
the bright calligraphy
of cloud on sky is swept aside
until all the mind's eye can see …

… is the soft machine of the lake starting up,
and, slowly emerging from fog,
the tree line, the chimneys, the Big House itself,
and these figures I've long come to love:

the jogger facing her long road alone,
the young mother on the school run,
the post man bringing news of the world,
of things done, and so much undone.

This morning there's sunshine and promise,
but even when frost grips these fields
the battered statues of Emo Court
are out here to practise Tai Chi.

One has an elbow that's bare to the bone,
others are fresh amputees,
yet nothing – not weather, not worries, not woes –
prevents them from practising Tai Chi.

Through hardships nigh unimaginable,
through insult and injury
the plaster statues of Emo Court
all the while practise Tai Chi.

2

I CAME HERE first with my mother,
that seems a lifetime ago.
Then slowly our roles were exchanged as we strolled.
When I looked she'd already grown old.

But the way she would stroke the cheeks of my boys,
both long since taller than me
in the blink of an eye, was a gesture distinct
as a movement out of Tai Chi.

And back in the days of the Big House itself,
the kitchens all bustle and steam,
the gardens rich with pheasant and fowl,
the lake full of rudd, perch and bream,

imagine the lady's maid sat up in bed,
the pantry girl roused from her sleep
slipping outside under cover of nightfall
to meet the young men of their dreams;

the treasures of empire heavy on shelves,
the brasses and trophies a-gleam,
while they danced in their night-shifts,
    or wished that they might,
like the statues that practise Tai Chi.

The Jesuits too in their time came and went,
the leaves shed by time's tree,
the statues consigned to the depths, so it's said,
holding their breath for years.

I've watched them since I can remember,
their poise, their fragility,
while we pass by in a relative blur
slaves to industry.

Some nights in a small frame of moonlight,
some days under inches of snow,
with nothing much other to do with their time,
and nowhere else to go,

spiders spinning webs in their limbs,
moss on their shoulders and knees,
as if dreaming the statues of Emo
patiently practise Tai Chi.

AND WHO CAN SAY what's in the future,
where the path up ahead might yet lead.
But the light will return to admire the resolve
of these statues that practise Tai Chi.

PAT BORAN is an Irish poet, fiction writer and, in recent times, short film maker. He is the author of more than a dozen books of poetry and prose, and is a member of Aosdána, Ireland's affiliation of creative artists. Born and raised in Portlaoise, he has written a great deal about the town and surrounding county over many years, most notably in his humorous memoir *The Invisible Prison: Scenes from an Irish Childhood*. Since he was a boy he has been a regular visitor to Emo Court and considers it one of the treasures of the Irish midlands. For more, see *www.patboran.com*.